METHAMPHETAMINE

SPEED KILLS

Methamphetamine is a powerfully addictive drug that speeds up a person's system. You risk your health by taking methamphetamine.

THE DRUG ABUSE PREVENTION LIBRARY

METHAMPHETAMINE

SPEED KILLS

Jay Schleifer

The Rosen Publishing Group, Inc.
NEW YORK

Published in 1999 by The Rosen Publishing Group, Inc.
29 East 21st Street, New York, NY 10010

First Edition 1999

Copyright © 1999 by The Rosen Publishing Group, Inc.

Library of Congress Cataloging-in-Publication Data
Schleifer, Jay.
   Methamphetamine: speed kills / Jay Schleifer
       p.   cm.—(The drug abuse prevention library)
   Includes bibliographical references and index.
   Summary: Discusses the drug methamphetamine, how it is used and abused, its effects, ways to avoid drug addiction, and how to get help for an addiction.
   ISBN 0-8239-2512-9
   1. Amphetamines—Juvenile literature. 2. Teenagers—Drug use—United States—Juvenile literature. 3. Drug abuse—United States—Prevention—Juvenile literature. [1. Methamphetamine. 2. Amphetamine. 3. Drug abuse.] I. Title. II. Series.
HV5822.A5S35 1998
362.29'9—dc21   98-45096
                                  CIP
                                   AC

Contents

Introduction

*T*om, a high-school senior, was depressed and bored after breaking up with his girlfriend. A friend offered help in the form of a white powder that had to be breathed in but, this friend promised, would take his problems away.

Tom was curious, but careful. Like many kids his age, he'd smoked a little pot, even though he thought it was risky. He also knew there were far more dangerous drugs around. Drugs that could hook you, if they didn't kill you.

"Is that crack?" he asked. "If it is, forget it!"

"Not at all," the friend assured him. "It's just something that will open you up a little, get you feeling good."

The friend was telling a partial truth. It wasn't crack, the smokable form of cocaine. But the friend was also misleading Tom. The *drug he was offering was a dangerous stimulant like crack.*

Tom took the bait, and the drug. The friend laid the powder out in two lines on a pocket mirror. Tom leaned down, closed his eyes, and snorted.

At first, the sting hitting his nostrils startled and scared him. But in seconds, he became aware of the most powerful sense of well-being he had ever felt.

Now Tom felt he had the power of ten, or maybe a hundred. His problems were suddenly just flecks of dust. Even better, the powerful feeling lasted for hours.

Over the next few days and weeks, Tom returned again and again for more of the magic powder. He found his need for it increasing. Each dose had to be larger for him to get the same rush.

But his friend was no longer giving him the drug. He was selling it. Tom was now spending about $100 for a week's worth. Money he had saved for college from his part-time job was paying for the drug.

Something else had changed. Tom had always been a nice, easygoing kid. Now, between hits, he was impossible to live with. He was fighting with both friends and loved ones, losing weight, sometimes going three days without sleep, and then crashing for twenty-four hours straight.

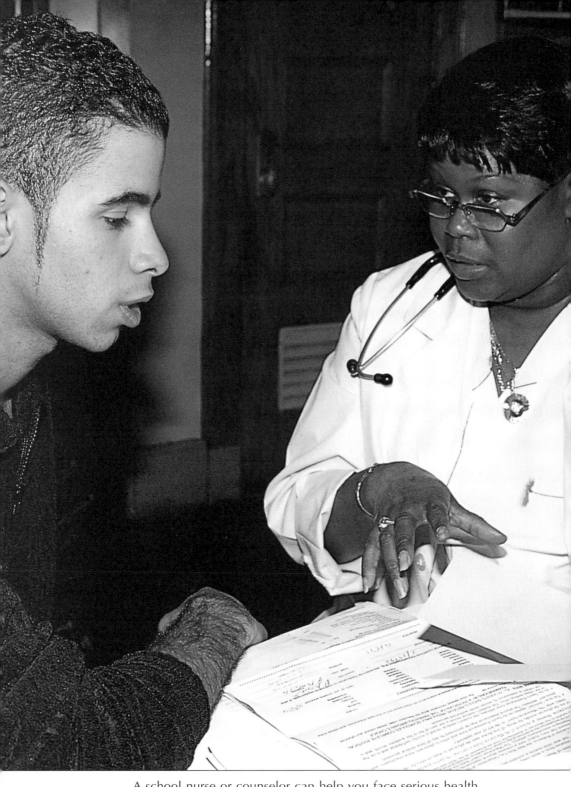

A school nurse or counselor can help you face serious health issues, such as an addiction to methamphetamine.

Even his appearance changed. Rashes had *begun to show up on his skin. They got worse with Tom's constant scratching of a terrible itch that no cream or lotion could stop. Then, after a terrible argument with his dad, Tom walked out of the house and didn't come back.*

No one knew where he was until the hospital called.

"Your son has been brought in with a bad infection," the doctors told Tom's parents. "His body can no longer fight off infection. Your son is dangerously ill." Ten days later he was dead.

What had killed Tom was a monster with many nicknames: speed, crystal, crystal meth, shabu, L.A. glass, ice. But there is only one official name: methamphetamine. Cheap, easy to make, and extremely powerful, this drug had killed teens before.

By sharing your thoughts and concerns with caring, supportive adults, you can make smart choices in life.

CHAPTER 1

The Need for Speed

Methamphetamine, or meth, comes from a class of drugs called stimulants. As the word suggests, these drugs stimulate, or speed up, both mental and physical processes. These processes include thinking, heart rate, blood pressure, and overall body activity.

History of Stimulants

The most commonly used stimulant is caffeine. A naturally occurring stimulant, caffeine is found in the everyday cup of coffee and can of cola. Caffeine provides the jump start for much of the American workforce each morning. Caffeine is also sold over the counter at drugstores in the pill form of non-sleep aids such as NoDoz.

12 There are a number of types of stimulants. Their nicknames include pep pills, bennies, uppers, and thrusters. Basic amphetamine was created in 1887, but the drug was not widely used until 1932. Then it was put on the market in an inhaler to help people with asthma breathe more easily by speeding up the opening of their air passageways.

During World War II (1939–1945), amphetamine use became widespread as pilots and soldiers took the drug in pill form to stay awake in battle. More than 180 million pills were used in this way.

After the war, truckers and pilots used the drug to keep going during long cross-country treks. But when the drug wore off, operators often fell asleep instantly, even when in midair flight or moving down the highway. After a series of widely reported accidents, operator use of amphetamine (while on the job) was banned.

In the 1950s, dieters began using amphetamine as a weight-loss drug. It was also used by college students for all-night study sessions and by athletes to improve performance. But in the 1960s, people began to use amphetamine as a recreational drug, along with pot and other drugs such as LSD. Many people died from overdoses.

During World War II, many soldiers used amphetamine to stay alert over long periods of time.

Street Names

Meth comes in several forms and has several nicknames:

- The original form is a pill called Methedrine.

- The version that is snorted is a white powder called crank. Other street names for the drug are zip, go-fast, cristy, and chalk. Crank can also be mixed with water and injected with a needle. Sometimes crank is mixed with crack cocaine; the result is called croak.

- A version that can be heated in a pipe and smoked is known as crystal or crystal meth.

- The newest form of meth is a superpure version that is smoked in a pipe. In this form, the drug looks like little chips of ice. For that reason, it has the nicknames ice, glass, and crystal.

Methamphetamine was created by Japanese chemists in 1919. Since the 1960s, its use has steadily gained popularity and in the 1990s has exploded. Today, meth is often used by kids who go to raves—all-night parties that sometimes go on for days, taking place in clubs and empty warehouses. Ravers usually range in age from twelve or thirteen to twenty-five. At raves, meth, acid (LSD), and Ecstasy (MDMA) are passed around like candy. Meth is the drug of choice for those who want the stamina to stay awake and dance until sunrise (and often beyond).

Meth vs. Cocaine

Some Americans use meth as a substitute for cocaine for several reasons. Cocaine produces an intense high that lasts just minutes or an hour; the user must take hits many times a day to stay high. Meth produces a similar or stronger high, but one hit can last for several hours. The user needs less of the drug to stay high.

Cocaine (coke) is expensive, although crack, the smokable form, costs less than the powder form. An average day's supply can cost about $100. For this reason, coke has always been thought of as a rich man's drug. In comparison, meth is cheap. For

Teens often take meth at all-night dance parties for extra stamina.

the same $100, a user can get enough meth 17
for an entire week. Meth has been called
"poor man's cocaine."

Both drugs can be injected, snorted, or
smoked. But because meth is cheaper,
easier to get, and produces effects similar
to those of cocaine, its use is skyrocketing.
And so are the problems it brings.

CHAPTER 2

Speed Bumps

*O*ne of the major problems with methamphetamine is how and where it is made. Methamphetamine labs are dirty, foul-smelling chemical mills hidden in remote areas to prevent discovery. The operators lack training and care little about the quality of the product or the health of those who will use it. Their sole concern is making money.

The chemicals used are both flammable and explosive. Meth labs blow up regularly, taking their operators' lives. In one case, a man ran a lab in his home. When the lab went up, the operator, his wife, and three young children died.

The process of manufacturing methamphetamine is extremely risky. Meth is made

Methamphetamine is manufactured in unsafe labs, often with poisonous, flammable chemicals.

by "cooking" several deadly chemicals together. A small error in the formula or use of chemicals that are either old or impure can result in the death of anyone using the product.

The Meth Business

In the United States, the business of making meth is moving from the West Coast to the East Coast. Use of the drug has always been strongest in California and the Southwest. (San Diego has been the United States' speed capital for years.) But by the mid-1990s, meth use had begun to spread across the country.

This was partly because East Coast cocaine kings were said to be fighting to

20 protect their market from the new, cheaper product. In California and southwestern cities, doctors know more about meth than they'd ever want to. Between 1991 and 1994, meth-related problems in San Diego emergency rooms doubled. And four of every ten male suspects booked at county jails tested positive for meth.

But the same alarming increases are now showing up in other parts of the country. The jail in Jasper County, Iowa, holds just twenty-four inmates, but 90 percent have problems with meth.

In the United States, a person needs a government permit to buy from U.S. companies the chemicals needed to make meth. But they can still be bought without a permit in other countries. Chemicals are often brought over the U.S. border, and the meth is then manufactured in American labs.

Pushing Meth

All versions of methamphetamine go from the lab to a distribution network, and then to the dealers who sell the drug on the street. Along the way, these middlepeople "cut" the meth by mixing it with other chemicals. This increases their supply of the drug so that they will have more to sell to users and make more money. The materials used in cutting vary widely—cornstarch, *21* baby laxatives, baking soda, even rat poison. Methamphetamine itself is often used to cut cocaine or heroin. Users never know what they are getting when they buy drugs.

Meth users have home-brewed their own versions of meth. During the early 1990s, for example, speed users in the Midwest dreamed up something they called CAT, short for the chemical name methacathinone. In place of the hard-to-get chemicals used in cooking up regular meth, CAT-makers substituted whatever they had readily available. The recipe called for, among other things, household drain cleaner and battery acid.

Problems of a Superstimulant

All drugs change a person's body chemistry. But meth is the most powerful of stimulants. It overwhelms the brain and nervous system.

You may already know that the brain operates by sending signals between clusters of nerve cells. These signals are often imagined as flashes of lightning inside the skull. But in fact, the signals are liquid chemicals sent from signaling cells and soaked up by receiving cells. The chemicals stimulate the receiving cells to action.

Quickly absorbed into the brain, meth

When something good happens, such as having fun with friends, the body naturally releases a chemical called dopamine. Dopamine induces a feeling of happiness.

mixes with this outgoing and incoming chemical tide. The meth allows chemicals to leave the signaling cells, but blocks them from soaking into the receiving cells. As a result, the sending cells pump out more chemicals. Within seconds, the brain is awash in stimulants.

Meth seems to have the greatest effect on the brain by increasing the production of a very important natural chemical stimulant called dopamine. This substance is involved with thinking, emotions such as happiness, and feelings of energy. It also plays a part in controlling body movement.

As the brain of a meth user produces more and more dopamine, the drug user starts to feel larger than life, happy to the *23* point of giddiness, capable of incredible feats of strength, beautiful, full of wisdom, and daring. There seems to be nothing he or she cannot do.

Yet these feelings are an illusion. They are caused by a reaction to the drug. Scientists have tested users to see if their abilities actually increase while they are on meth. Some tests show improvement in some areas. But the improvement, if any, is only slight. It is certainly nowhere near what the user believes it to be.

Meanwhile, observers see the user as hyper, even crazed. His or her body twitches and jerks, and speech may seem like nothing more than babble. Even the most basic tasks become a challenge. Users are unable to eat and sleep normally, much less complete or focus clearly on any task. Based on this behavior, the term often used to describe them is "speed freaks."

Crashing and Tweaking

The meth high wears off in four to twenty-four hours, depending on the strength of the dose. And with meth, the crash is terrible.

As the drug wears off, the process of over-stimulation begins to run in reverse. The brain begins to produce less dopamine, and

Meth offers people feelings of power and strength, but when its effects wear off, users experience painful withdrawal symptoms.

cells that were once flush with dopamine |
begin to react as if deprived.

The user feels depressed, unhappy, and often physically sick. He or she experiences sweats, violent behavior, sleeplessness, and terrible bouts of itching, as if bugs were crawling on the skin.

In order to avoid the painful process of coming down, meth abusers often use continuously and may go for days without sleep. This pattern is called "tweaking." After tweaking, users experience an even harder crash.

"I would have these out-of-body experiences," said seventeen-year-old Erin Smith of Las Lomas, California, in Time Out *magazine. "I would try to scream at the top of my lungs. But only little squeaks would come out."*

"I got so tweaked out I'd see heads popping out of the walls, and I'd go chase them," reported another meth user in the same Time Out *article.*

Over time, so much damage may be done to the mind and body that these effects never fully go away. A user may feel threatened by imaginary demons, for example, even when he or she has not used the drug for some time.

Effects of Meth
A Catalog of Consequences

The National Drug and Alcohol Treatment Referral Routing Service recently compiled this summary of the dangerous health effects of meth:

SHORT-TERM EFFECTS

increased alertness
sense of well-being
paranoia
intense high
hallucinations
increased heart rate
convulsions
extreme rise in body temperature

uncontrollable movements
violent behavior
insomnia (inability to sleep)
impaired speech
dry, itchy skin
loss of appetite
acne, sores
numbness

EFFECTS ON THE MIND

disturbed sleep
excessive excitation
excessive talking
panic
anxiety
nervousness
moodiness and irritability

false sense of confidence and power
delusions of grandeur
lack of interest in friends, food, or sex
aggressive and violent behavior
severe depression

WITHDRAWAL SYMPTOMS

severe cravings
insomnia
restlessness
mental confusion

depression
itching
sweats
violent behavior

LONG-TERM EFFECTS

fatal kidney and lung disorders
brain damage

depression
hallucinations
disorganized lifestyle

Physical Effects of Meth

Meth attacks the mind as well as the body. As the drug kicks a person's body systems into hyperdrive, heart rate and blood pressure skyrocket. Body temperature can soar as high as 108 degrees, hot enough to destroy delicate cells. The body may go into shaking fits called convulsions.

High blood pressure is especially danger-ous if a person has an aneurysm, the medical term for a weak spot in a major blood vessel. It is possible to live a normal, healthy life without ever knowing the weakness is there, since normal blood pressure may not be high enough to break through. But when meth sends an intense surge of blood into the spot, the vessel can burst. Nearby tissue is flooded while blood no longer reaches cells farther down the line. If this happens in the brain, the user may have a stroke.

Stroke victims often lose their powers of speech, eyesight, and motion. They can lose the use of an entire side of their body, or even go into a coma. If the stroke occurs at the brain's control center for breathing or heartbeat, death may follow. Even if a meth user's blood vessels are strong, the heart may begin to beat irregularly or simply burst from overstimulation, with the same lethal result.

Many dangerous health problems can result from methamphetamine use.

If the user survives these immediate dangers, long-term harm may still occur. It is the job of the liver and kidneys to help process chemicals entering the body and to rid the blood of toxic substances. When meth flows through these organs, it destroys key cells. The user loses some of the ability to fight infection. He or she may die from a simple case of the flu or a bad cold.

The nose, throat, and lungs may also be damaged by breathing in meth's powerful chemicals. And with injected meth comes the danger all drug users face from dirty or shared needles—contracting HIV, the virus that causes AIDS.

These dangers multiply when the user chooses ice. More than 90 percent of each ice pellet is pure methamphetamine. The more meth in the dose, the higher the risk of damage to key body systems.

Speed really does kill. Between 1991 and 1994, deaths from meth tripled nationwide. In some cities, they have risen to two to five times what they were just a few years ago. Some deaths were from overdoses. Others were suicides caused by the potent powers of meth. From 1989 to 1995, emergency room visits involving meth abuse doubled. In 1996, twice as many high school seniors reported having tried crystal meth than in 1990.

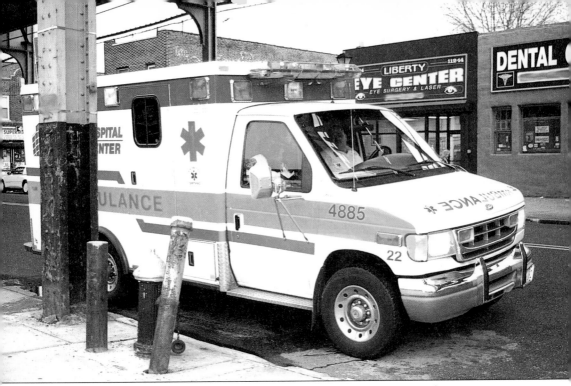

Emergency room visits involving methamphetamine abuse are on the rise.

Even when meth doesn't kill, users turn control of their lives over to the drug. Meth addiction is powerful and quick.

Psychological Effects of Meth

Meth use causes psychological addiction: Users mentally crave the drug. These cravings can be overwhelming. While users may miss the high between hits, the crash they experience is psychologically disturbing. "Coming off the drug is really bad," says Dr. Raymond Manning, who works with meth cases in Pasadena, California. "Users tend to do more meth rather than go through coming down again."

When users return to the drug, they often find that the physical price of their addiction has risen. The body develops a tolerance for meth. That means the amount they originally took no longer has the same effect. Users must then take more of the drug to get the same high. Once hooked, they have no easy way out.

Because meth is so strong, it doesn't take much for young people to get hooked. Users find themselves addicted in as little as four months. Dealers know this and are happy to offer a "free trial supply" or low prices. The dealers know the person will lose control and become addicted.

What is life like for a meth abuser? One nameless addict left this "poem" on an Internet bulletin board:

It's time to get some sleep when:
--You're out of crank
--Your face is bouncing off the table
--Your veins have disappeared beneath
    pasty gooseflesh
--Your shoes don't fit anymore
--24 projects you've started all stall at once
--Everyone is a cop
--You've just set yourself on fire... again.
                        "Speed Phreak"

CHAPTER 3

Stopped for Speeding

*I*n high school, *Janet was known as the* *"Everything Girl." She was beautiful, super* *smart, and at the helm of every club in school.* *She greeted everyone with a smile and was* *voted "Most Likely to Realize Her Dreams."* *In the early fall of her freshman year at the* *state university, she met Keith. He fit the profile* *of the perfect boyfriend: cute, intelligent, and* *politically active. He was what she thought* *she'd always dreamed of.*

After they had been dating for three weeks, *Janet began to get a little jealous of Keith. It* *wasn't that he was interested in other girls, it* *was because his energy seemed endless. He rarely* *slept. When Janet asked if life had always been* *this easy for him, he avoided the question. She* *had also noticed that he was getting skinnier,*

that he often twitched for no apparent reason, **33**
and that he was more paranoid than anyone she
had ever known. Janet tried not to think about
it because it only upset her.

One Thursday night, Janet went to a house
party thrown by a bunch of Keith's friends.
Keith introduced her to a guy named Doug,
whom Keith had never mentioned before. Janet
thought Doug was the strangest guy she had
ever met. He was constantly looking around the
room as they talked, and he wore dark sun-
glasses, even though it was almost midnight.

Doug whispered something into Keith's ear.
Then the two of them started down the base-
ment stairs. Janet called out to Keith, and he
said he would be right back. Although she sus-
pected something dangerous, Janet demanded
to know what was going on. Keith took her
aside as Doug stood at the top of the stairs
looking impatient, annoyed, and freaked out.

Keith said, "Listen, I was gonna save this
as a surprise for our one-month anniversary,
but if you insist, you can get in on it now." He
smiled and took her hand as he led her down
the stairs. On the dimly lit stairwell, he passed
her the pipe that Doug had carefully lit. Before
she could hand it back to Doug and tell Keith
that she never wanted to see him again, the
basement door opened and three cops had her
and the guys up against the wall. It didn't

34 *matter to the cops that she was a straight-A student, the daughter of proud parents, and what most people would call a "good kid." All that mattered now was that she held a controlled substance in her hand.*

Janet's life was forever changed by her arrest. Her lawyers couldn't wipe her record clean. The fact that she had been arrested for possession would stay with her for the rest of her life. It might prevent her from becoming a lawyer, a doctor, or a teacher. Whatever dreams she'd had as an adolescent might be shattered by the time she spent with a meth user.

If mental breakdown or bad health doesn't get you, the law probably will. Methamphetamine is a federally controlled substance. That means it is illegal for anyone to have or use it except medical professionals licensed to prescribe it. It is a Schedule II drug under federal regulations, which means that it has a high potential for abuse with a strong tendency to cause dependence. If you're caught carrying enough meth to sell, and don't have an M.D. after your name, you are looking at five to ten years in a federal prison. Even if you have just a small amount for personal use, you can still be looking at a $10,000 civil fine.

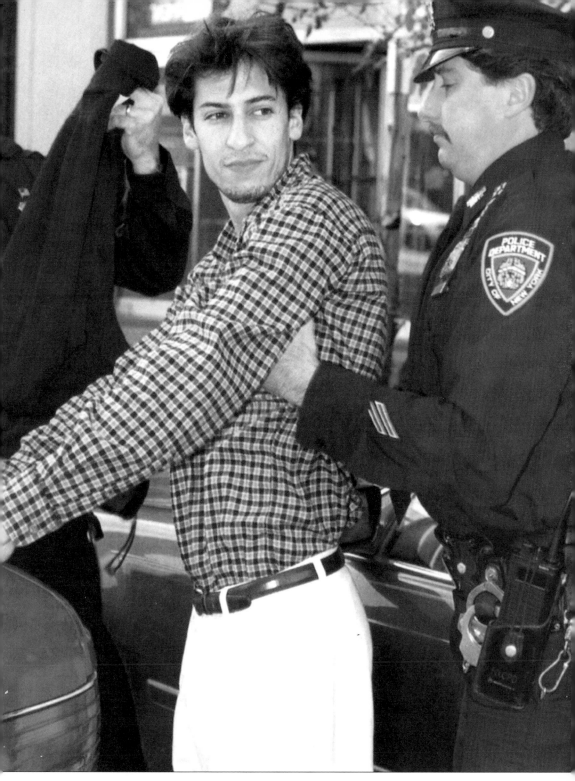

Using or selling methamphetamine is illegal, and people who are caught risk going to jail.

36 Of course, once a user has a criminal record, it can become difficult to land a decent job or get certain government benefits. If you're beginning to think it's just not worth it, you're in good company.

Meth makers and pushers get caught. When the drugs are made in labs, a strong odor is released, and that smell can travel long distances. Police use drug-detector dogs and aircraft to detect the highly visible fumes. Meanwhile, computers track the sale of the chemicals needed to make meth, and undercover agents join the gangs that make and transport the drug. Drug Enforcement Agency (DEA) and police forces gather information on lab location, weapons on site, and other matters to plan massive raids that catch the drug dealers.

Users get caught, too. One current police trend is to plant young-looking officers in the schools or on the street corners where users make their buys. Users are often videotaped as they hand over their cash to an undercover agent and pocket what looks like the drug (it's often harmless cornstarch or even crushed nuts posing as the smokable form). "The same hand that turns over your 'paper' of crank may then slap handcuffs on your wrists," says one undercover agent.

Using computer technology, law-enforcement officials can track the sale of chemicals needed to make methamphetamine.

The meth battle is being fought locally and nationally. In 1996, President Clinton worked with drug enforcement experts to devise a new strategy to stop the spread of meth. Some of his goals were to:

- Motivate America's youth to reject drugs by expanding the Safe and Drug-Free School program.
- Reduce drug- and crime-related violence. The 1994 Crime Bill put 100,000 new cops on the streets. The administration has expanded drug treatment for addicts and has developed a drug-testing program for all federal arrestees to help end the cycle of violence and drug abuse.

38

- Control U.S. borders through initiatives such as "Operation Hard Line" of the United States' Bureau of Customs. The increased number of border patrols has also helped to close down the border to drug traffickers.

Speed Hurts Others

Speeding with meth can cost a user his or her freedom, his or her health, even his or her life. But incredible as it may seem, some addicts believe that their drug use is no one's business but their own. Who else is harmed, they ask? Doesn't every American have a right to make individual decisions if those decisions don't affect others? Perhaps. But meth use does affect others in these ways.

Accidents

High on speed, a user loses all judgment when controlling a motor vehicle or even walking down a street. Meth-heads believe nothing can harm them. They take incredible risks at high speeds, thinking they can beat trains at railroad crossings, drive for hours past the point of exhaustion, or even run out into traffic, daring passing motorists to hit them. The resulting accidents can kill or maim not only the user but those in other vehicles.

Crime

Although meth is fairly cheap compared to cocaine and other hard drugs, users still need fast cash to feed their habit. This may lead to theft, burglary, or even armed robbery.

Fires and Explosions

Meth is made by combining flammable and explosive chemicals. The labs that make the drug seldom have safety controls or fire safety equipment. Explosions are common. Many labs operate in remote areas, but they have also been set up in houses in crowded inner cities. If an urban lab blows up, many innocent people could die.

Risk to the Unborn

If a pregnant woman uses meth, she is likely to harm her unborn child. The chance of birth defects is heightened. Meth babies often suffer shaking fits and may cry nonstop for twenty-four hours. Often, as these babies grow, they fail to develop normally.

Hazardous Waste

Many chemical processes, including the making of meth, produce poisonous waste material as a by-product. Responsible chemical manufacturing companies have their wastes carefully trucked away to be

If meth is made in a densely populated area, it can pose a threat to people who live nearby.

recycled, burned, or buried in a safe and approved manner. Because meth labs are illegal, they leave the chemicals behind to poison the soil or water supply or harm animals or people that live in the area.

Costs to Society

Drug abuse impacts society. For example, meth addiction can cause poverty if users lose their jobs or deplete the family savings to pay for drugs. These users may then require welfare or even costly emergency treatment, which must be paid for by publicly funded hospitals. Crimes such as burglary and assault are also associated with drug addiction. The cost for law enforcement, judges, and prisons is expensive.

Totaling the cost of methamphetamine 41 abuse alone is difficult. But government leaders have estimated that the overall cost for illegal drug use in the United States is more than $100 billion a year.

Loved Ones Pay the Highest Price

The greatest cost may be to the families and friends of the user. An addict's loved ones go through a confusing and painful time in which everything they thought they knew about the person suddenly doesn't apply.

This is especially true of meth users. Almost from the first hit, the drug creates basic and sudden changes in someone's personality and life patterns.

- A user may lose all interest in lifelong relationships, becoming hostile and even violent to friends and family.
- Life patterns change. A user may disappear all night, or for several nights, and then come home and "crash," sleeping for twenty-four hours straight.
- Favorite foods, sports, and hobbies are no longer of interest. Binge eating may follow several days of going without much food. The user may also become extremely thirsty.

- The user may refuse to talk about these changes, becoming angry and abusive if pressed on the matter.
- Schoolwork patterns may change. Grades may actually improve slightly due to bursts of energy from the first few experiences with meth. But in the long run, grades suffer as homework and study are neglected and the user falls into depression. Long-held goals such as going to college just don't matter anymore.
- Petty theft may arise as the user needs to scrape together cash for the next hit. This may lead to more serious crimes, such as burglary or robbery.
- Appearance is likely to change. Sudden loss of as much as ten to fifteen pounds a month is not unusual among female meth users. (Some may take the drug for that very reason.) Scars and rashes may also appear on the skin, aggravated by constant scratching.

Parents may realize that something is wrong with their child but not know what it is. Parents often don't know what to look for. If they try to sniff out a telltale odor in a child's room or on his or her breath, they

Changes in a teen's behavior may warn parents of a possible drug problem. Parents may confront the teen with their suspicions.

won't find one. Although the processing of meth causes a foul stench, the finished product gives off no odor when used. And personal supplies of meth are small and easily hidden. Because the drug does not need to be injected, no needles will be lying around. The most likely evidence may be a small glass pipe, which is also easy to hide.

"I just didn't know what it was," recalls the mother of one meth abuser. "I'd stay up and wait for him to come home and assess him. I especially dreaded the weekends."

When some parents find out the type of problem they are facing, they refuse to accept the fact. Maureen Ketchum, who heads an antidrug program in Marin County, California, reports, "One mother told me

44 | speed was no different than the caffeine pills they sold down at the 7-Eleven."

More often, parents spend the rest of their lives blaming themselves. "I feel like I failed my son," said one father who lost a son to methamphetamine. "He was a really good kid, even though he made some wrong decisions. And the drug just sucked him away."

Why Do People Use Meth?

Given the risks, it's fair to ask why young people would want to pump these poisons into their bodies. It should come as no surprise that their answers are no different from the reasons given for other forms of teen drug abuse:

Escape

During the teen years, we experience pressure from school, family, and romantic attachments. Drugs seem to offer an escape from worries, if only for a little while. A teen thinks he or she can temporarily drop out of the real world to what seems a better place.

Pleasure

There's no getting around it. At first, meth can make a user feel better than he or she has ever felt before—brilliant, powerful, and fearless. However, any apparent change in ability is minor and temporary.

"Because My Friends Do It!"

Peer pressure is one of the most powerful influences in a teen's life. Its effects are usually seen in the desire to wear the same clothes or listen to the same music friends do. But if those friends are "amping" on speed, the teen may feel pressure to follow them.

It is also important to realize that some teens use peer pressure for their own ends. They make money selling drugs to friends, which both finances their own habit and puts a lot of cash in their pockets. The drug sellers also gain power in the peer group, getting first choice of the best seat in the car or spot on the corner or the prettiest girl or handsomest guy to date.

"Because My Family Does It!"

Some teens think that if a close relative does drugs, they're fated to do the same. It is true that some people are predisposed to addiction because of their genes. But genetic makeup can never make someone start taking any of these substances. You always have control over your actions. In fact, knowing that your family includes

46 people with addictions should make you more careful about what you choose to do.

Fear

Illegal drugs are big business, and in some cases, dealers actually threaten young people who refuse to get involved with them. When this happens, it's time to call for help!

No one wants to rat on a friend or fellow student, but your school security personnel or local police can take action against a dangerous bully who is also a drug pusher. Talk to a trusted adult if you're not sure what to do.

It may be a greater danger to become involved with drug dealers. Doing what they tell you will not make them less violent. In fact, it will encourage them to scale up their tactics until a victim is badly hurt. That victim could be you!

CHAPTER 4

Speed Limits

*T*he bad news about meth use is that it's spreading. The good news is that users can stop if their addiction is caught in time. Unlike heroin and some other drugs, meth makes no permanent changes in the user's body chemistry. Once the drug is out of the system, it's out. A user may have a psychological craving for more, but the body will function without the drug.

The tough problem is dealing with the user's mind. The help of either a counselor or a mental health professional is often required. The longer a person has been on the drug, the harder the task of breaking free will be. Following are steps to take to deal with meth addiction.

Finding Help

If you or someone you love is abusing

Talking to a counselor may be the first step in overcoming an addiction.

meth, the worst thing you can do is deny the problem. Talk to a parent, a school guidance counselor, the family doctor, or another responsible adult. He or she may help you or your loved one get started on the road to recovery.

Hotlines

There are several hotlines to call for information about getting help. These hotlines usually do not require you to leave your name. The national hotline is the National Drug and Alcohol Treatment Referral Routing Service at (800) 662-HELP (4357). This organization can supply:

• Printed materials

- A description of the types of treat- **49**
  ment services available in your state
- Referrals to treatment for multiple
  addictions such as abuse of both
  speed and alcohol
- Information about general teen and
  family support services in your state

Numerous state, city, and private hotlines
are listed in the phone book or are available
through information operators. State and
local services are usually connected with the
Department of Public Health or Department of Mental Health. Your best source of
help, though, may be a school counselor. He
or she will know whom to call and how to
get help while protecting your rights of
privacy and confidentiality in the process.

Recovery
Recovery is a three-step process. A person
will go through:

- Detoxification
- Rehabilitation
- Aftercare

Detoxification is a medical procedure
that helps a person through withdrawal. He
or she will be under medical care during

50 this time. He or she may be assigned a trained counselor and a "buddy." A buddy is another patient who has already completed detoxification. These people provide a person in recovery with encouragement and support during this portion of the treatment process. Detoxification may last between two and four days.

Rehabilitation takes place in a treatment center and provides a protected and controlled environment that allows a person time to accept his or her disease. This involves activities designed to modify the addicted person's lifestyle. A person recovering from addiction must follow a specified daily routine. These practices are designed to help the person develop a healthier way of life, learn self-discipline, and take responsibility for his or her well-being. This process may take up to thirty days.

Aftercare begins when the person leaves the treatment center and returns to his or her home environment. Participation in support group meetings, which began during treatment, is now part of the daily routine. Attending these support group meetings is essential for recovery.

During recovery a person may attend and follow a Twelve Step program. Alcoholics Anonymous created the first Twelve

Support groups can help people in recovery learn new solutions to problems.

Step program. Now several exist. These programs help people in recovery understand why they turned to drugs and alcohol, and that addiction is a disease. A person will learn how to face problems without turning to drugs and how to avoid returning to his or her old way of life. The following organizations have Twelve Step programs:

- Alcoholics Anonymous (AA)
- Narcotics Anonymous (NA)
- Cocaine Anonymous (CA)
- Al-Anon—support group for families of substance abusers
- Alateen—support group for teenagers in families of substance abusers

52 | ## Factors That Affect Recovery

Experts at rehabilitation centers have looked into what makes the difference between success and failure in breaking the addiction to meth and other drugs. These are their criteria for success:

How serious the teen is about quitting.
Rehab is a tough process. If the teen has any doubt about why it is needed and doesn't really believe he or she has a problem, the process will fail. Teens need to fully understand what drugs are doing to them and sincerely want to recover from their addiction.

How serious parents are about helping.
The teen's family cannot come into the program thinking that the treatment center will do all the work and they can just pick up their recovered son or daughter in a few weeks or months. Some centers will not admit a teen user unless his or her parents agree to come in as often as needed to join in the treatment process.

Staying away from drugs—and drug triggers.
In recovery, teens are taught to avoid the triggers, such as stress or peer pressure, that were their signals to take drugs. They

need to stay away from the people, places, and things they were around during their addiction. That may mean changing schools, dropping former after-school interests, and, hardest of all, giving up longtime friends. But new supportive friends are made, and they can help former addicts stay on the road to recovery. Both recovering addicts and their families also need to be aware that there may be temptations to get involved with other kinds of drugs, including alcohol. An addictive personality remains an addictive personality for life.

Roberta grew up in a neighborhood where drug addiction was as common as morning coffee. She had climbed over sleeping addicts and dirty needles on her way to school for years. Her mother constantly spoke of the perils of drug addiction. Roberta's father had died of a heroin overdose several years earlier. That's why her addicted brother Rich no longer lived with them. Her mother couldn't deal with watching the slow death of another person she loved.

Everyone thought Roberta was a good kid, but she was often depressed and felt like giving up. She daydreamed all the time, imagining what it would be like if she could escape her

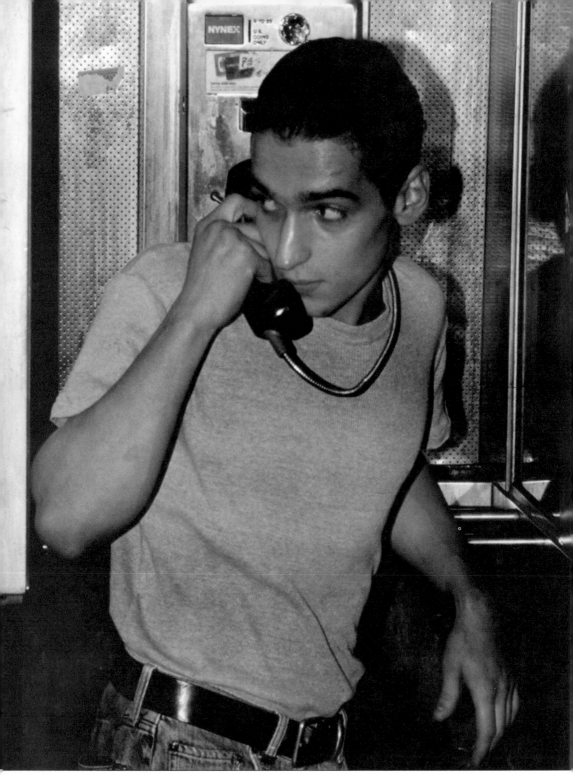

Help for methamphetamine addiction is often just a phone call away.

life. Something had been missing ever since Rich had left home years earlier.

Suddenly one night in June, Rich appeared in the living room. He was sitting on the couch watching television when Roberta came home from a late-night basketball game. He looked skinny and sick, and when Roberta went over and hugged him, he stared straight ahead blankly. "I've come home to die with you and Mom," he said, starting to sob. He clutched Roberta's shirt and cried, "I can't get off. It's too strong for me." Roberta knew her brother was talking about meth.

Roberta and her mom knew about Rich's meth addiction only because the treatment center in Ohio where he had ended up had called to let them know he was alive. When he first left home, he had been using crack. Now, four years later, Rich had relapsed again. But finally Roberta felt hope. Rich had returned home. It was the first time in years he had made contact. It meant that he wanted to heal, to finally kick the addiction.

Roberta had the address and phone number of a treatment center stored away, waiting for just this occasion. She knew that if he stayed at home to heal, with the temptation of drug addiction beckoning out on the city streets, Rich would get nowhere. She looked into her brother's eyes and told him, "You are not going

56 | *to die, Rich. I'm right here, and Mom's had enough time to deal with this. We're ready to help you. Are you ready to be helped?"*

"I think so," said Rich, almost inaudibly. His breath came fast and heavy. He was shaking. Roberta held him.

After three weeks at a rehab center upstate, Rich looked much better than on the day he came home. He still had a long way to go in his treatment, but he felt that recovery was possible for the first time. His mom and sister visited him at the facility once a week. He was starting to read the newspapers again. He knew that when he returned to the real world he would have to stay away from temptation. But he also knew that having his family as a support system would make it easier. He would have to work to stay off meth for the rest of his life, but he finally understood that his world could eventually be happy and full without drugs.

There's no easy success in recovery. Almost no one recovers without a few missteps along the way. Especially during the first three months of being off meth, a teen may again become depressed, moody, or violent. Both teens and their families need to be ready to forgive and continue with the recovery process when this happens.

Whatever it takes to beat meth, even abusers agree that it's worth the effort. "Speed is evil," says one longtime meth user. "I have seen more people's lives twisted up by that drug than by anything else in the world."

Glossary

abuse Misuse of a drug leading to harmful physical and psychological consequences.

addiction The condition of being unable to stop taking a drug.

amphetamine A group of powerful stimulants that speed up the body's central nervous system.

amping Getting a high from methamphetamine.

aneurysm A weak spot in a blood vessel.

CAT A home-brewed version of methamphetamine.

coma A condition of deep unconsciousness.

convulsion Involuntary, often violent muscle spasms or series of spasms.

crack Purified cocaine in chip form and
  used for smoking.

crash To come down off a drug experience.

crystal Powdered methamphetamine
  used for smoking.

methamphetamine The most powerful
  of the stimulants.

rehabilitation A program designed to
  help users break free of drug abuse.

speed Nickname for methamphetamine
  and other stimulants.

speed freak Methamphetamine or other
  stimulant abuser.

stimulant A drug that speeds up the
  central nervous system, impacting both
  mind and body.

stroke Massive rupture or obstruction of
  an artery in the brain.

tolerance The body's ability to get used
  to or become less responsive to a drug,
  requiring larger doses to get the same
  effect.

Where to Go for Help

Families Anonymous
P.O. Box 3475
Culver City, CA 90231
(800) 736-9805

Hazelden
C03, P.O. Box 11
Center City, MN 55012
Info Center
(800) 257-7810 (in U.S.)
(651) 257-4010 (outside U.S.)
Web site: http://www.hazelden.org

Nar-Anon Family Group Headquarters, Inc.
P.O. Box 2562
Palos Verdes Peninsula, CA 90274
(310) 547-5800

Narcotics Anonymous (NA)
World Service Office
P.O. Box 9999
Van Nuys, CA 91409
(818) 773-9999

Web site: http://www.na.org

National Clearinghouse for Alcohol and Drug
  Information
P.O. Box 2345
Rockville, MD 20847-2345
(800) 729-6686
Web site: http://www.health.org

National Council on Alcoholism and Drug
  Dependence
12 West 21st Street, 7th Floor
New York, NY 10010
(800) NCA-CALL (will refer you to your local
  treatment information center)
Web site: http://www.ncadd.org

Women for Sobriety
P.O. Box 618
Quakertown, PA 18951
(800) 333-1606
Web site: http://www.mediapulse.com/wfs

The National Drug and Alcohol Treatment
  Referral Routing Service
(800) 662-HELP (662-4357)

In Canada

Family Services Youth Detox Program
4305 St. Catherine's Street
Vancouver, BC V5V 4M4
(604) 872-4349

Narcotics Anonymous
P.O. Box 5700
Depot A
Toronto, ON M5W 1N9
(416) 691-9519

For Further Reading

Clayton, Lawrence, Ph.D. *Amphetamines and Other Stimulants.* Rev ed. New York: The Rosen Publishing Group, 1997.

Moser, Leslie E., Ph.D. *Crack, Cocaine, Methamphetamine, and Ice.* Waco, TX: Multi-Media Productions, Inc., 1990.

Nagle, Jeanne. *Everything You Need to Know About Drug Addiction.* New York: The Rosen Publishing Group, 1999.

Roberts, Todd C. "Built for Speed." *URB Magazine*, October 1995.

Wesson, Donald R., M.D., et al. *Crack and Ice: Treating Smokeable Stimulant Abuse.* Center City, MN: Hazelden Educational Materials, 1992.

Index

About the Author

Jay Schleifer is former editor of *Know Your World Extra,* a national classroom publication for teenage students. He has written more than forty books for teens. He is currently a publishing consultant and freelance author. He lives in the Midwest.

Photo Credits

Cover photo © Brian Silak; pp. 2, 8, 22, 24, 28, 40, 43, 48, 51, 54 by Ira Fox; pp. 10, 16, 37, by Seth Dinnerman; pp. 13, 19 © Corbis; p. 30 by Les Mills; p. 35 © AP/Wide World.